COIN COLLECTI

Your Complete Guide to Building, Valuing, and Profiting from Coin Collections

Alex Coinman

FOR THE FIRST 100 ONLY

CLAIM YOUR BONUS

NOW

Table of Contents

CHAPTER 1: INTRODUCTION TO COIN COLLECTING 3
THE FASCINATION OF COIN COLLECTING 3
SETTING YOUR COIN COLLECTING GOALS 6

CHAPTER 2: GETTING STARTED 9
BUILDING YOUR NUMISMATIC KNOWLEDGE 9
ASSEMBLING YOUR COIN COLLECTING TOOLKIT 13

CHAPTER 3: IDENTIFYING COINS 18
COIN TYPES AND VARIETIES 18
Building Your Collection with Intention 21
Strategies for Building a Diverse Collection 21
THE ART OF COIN IDENTIFICATION 22

CHAPTER 4: VALUING YOUR COLLECTION 27
FACTORS AFFECTING COIN VALUE 27
APPRAISAL AND VALUATION METHODS 31

CHAPTER 5: CURATING AND PRESERVING 37
COIN STORAGE AND DISPLAY 37
CLEANING AND PRESERVATION TECHNIQUES 40

CHAPTER 6: PROFITING FROM COIN COLLECTING 46
BUYING AND SELLING COINS 46
STRATEGIES FOR MAXIMIZING RETURNS 51

CHAPTER 7: RARE COINS AND HISTORICAL SIGNIFICANCE 55
COINS WITH UNIQUE HISTORICAL CONTEXT 55
DECODING THE CULTURAL SIGNIFICANCE 60

CHAPTER 8: CONCLUSION AND NEXT STEPS 68
REFLECTING ON YOUR COIN COLLECTING JOURNEY 68
CONTINUING TO EXPAND YOUR COLLECTION 69

Chapter 1:

Introduction to Coin Collecting

In a world filled with digital transactions and virtual currencies, there exists a timeless hobby that connects us to the rich tapestry of history—the art of coin collecting. For centuries, numismatics, the study and collection of coins, has captivated the hearts and minds of enthusiasts around the globe. Beyond the tangible value of currency, coins serve as tangible artifacts, bearing witness to the socio-economic, political, and cultural landscapes of their time.

The Fascination of Coin Collecting

Coin collecting, or numismatics, stands as a captivating pursuit that transcends time, linking enthusiasts to the intricate threads of human history. The allure of this hobby lies not merely in the act of accumulating metallic discs, but in the stories each coin tells, the historical imprints it bears, and the cultural reflections it encapsulates.

Coin collecting is a journey through time, a tangible interaction with the past. The coins we collect are not just currency; they are artifacts that bear witness to the societies, empires, and civilizations that have shaped our world. Holding an ancient coin from Greece, for instance, allows us to connect with the intellectual and artistic achievements of a bygone era. Examining a coin from the Renaissance transports us to a time of profound cultural and scientific transformation.

What makes coin collecting truly enchanting is the diversity of coins available. Whether ancient or modern, each coin possesses a unique identity. Some collectors are drawn to the mystique of ancient coins, relishing the opportunity to hold a piece of history in their hands. Others find joy in the intricate designs of commemorative coins or the thrill of discovering rare and valuable pieces. The spectrum of options allows collectors to tailor their pursuits to their individual interests, creating a dynamic and personal engagement with numismatics.

The artistic evolution of coins further enhances their allure. From the simplicity of early mintings to the intricate designs of contemporary coins, the evolution of artistic expression is showcased through these small, metallic canvases. Coins provide a condensed visual history, reflecting the prevailing styles, ideologies, and technological advancements of the times in which they were minted. The beauty of a coin extends beyond its material value, encapsulating the aesthetic sensibilities of its era.

Yet, beyond the historical and artistic dimensions, coin collecting offers a sense of discovery and adventure. Enthusiasts may find themselves immersed in antique shops, attending coin shows, or exploring online markets, in pursuit of that elusive coin to complete a set or the excitement of stumbling upon a rare and valuable piece. The process of discovery is a continual source of satisfaction for collectors, keeping the hobby dynamic and imbued with a perpetual sense of anticipation.

As collectors delve deeper into the world of numismatics, they often find themselves captivated by the stories behind each coin. Every minting has a narrative to tell, whether it's the historical events surrounding its creation, the political climate of the time, or the symbolism embedded in its design. These stories transform coins from inanimate objects into living artifacts that carry the echoes of the past into the present.

Now, let's explore the allure of specific coins that have left an indelible mark on the world of numismatics:

1. **Ancient Greek Silver Tetradrachm:** Imagine holding in your hands a piece of Ancient Greece, a Silver Tetradrachm minted during the 6th to 4th centuries BCE. These coins, adorned with depictions of mythological figures and symbols of power, serve as portals to an era of philosophical enlightenment and artistic brilliance. The Tetradrachm not only embodies the economic systems of ancient Greek city-states but also reflects the values and cultural achievements of a civilization that laid the foundation for Western thought.

2. **Roman Denarius:** Transitioning to the heart of the Roman Empire, the Roman Denarius emerges as a coin of immense historical significance. Minted from the third century BCE to the third century CE, the Denarius was the backbone of Roman currency. Its iconic images, featuring the profiles of emperors and scenes of military triumphs, offer collectors a glimpse into the grandeur and power of ancient Rome. The Roman Denarius, beyond its monetary role, serves as a tangible link to the political and cultural evolution of one of history's most influential civilizations.

3. **Byzantine Solidus:** Journeying into the Byzantine era, we encounter the Byzantine Solidus, a gold coin that symbolizes the resilience of the Eastern Roman Empire. Minted from the 4th to the 15th century CE, the Solidus reflects the stability and endurance of Byzantine economic systems. With images of emperors and religious symbols, the Solidus offers collectors a unique perspective on the intersection of governance and faith in the Byzantine world. Possessing a Byzantine Solidus is akin to holding a piece of the empire's golden age, a testament to its enduring legacy.

Beyond the personal enjoyment, coin collecting fosters a sense of community among enthusiasts. Numismatic forums, local clubs, and coin shows provide platforms for collectors to share their experiences, knowledge, and passion. Networking with fellow collectors opens avenues for learning, trading, and expanding one's collection. The camaraderie forged within the numismatic community adds a social dimension to the hobby, creating connections that transcend geographical boundaries.

Setting foot into the world of coin collecting is not merely an act of amassing artifacts but an immersion into a hobby that combines history, art, and the joy of discovery. It is a journey where the past and present converge, and where each coin becomes a portal to a different time and place.

Setting Your Coin Collecting Goals

As you embark on this fascinating pursuit, establishing well-defined goals becomes a crucial aspect of ensuring a purposeful and enjoyable numismatic experience. Setting goals not only provides direction to your collection but also adds depth to your engagement with the diverse world of coins. Here, we will delve into the intricacies of setting coin collecting goals, offering insights and guidance to help you shape a meaningful and fulfilling numismatic journey.

1. **Define Your Focus:** The first step in setting coin collecting goals is to define your focus. Numismatics encompasses a vast array of coins, from ancient to modern, with diverse themes and historical significance. Consider what specifically captivates your interest. Are you drawn to ancient civilizations, medieval coinage, or modern commemorative issues? Defining your focus will not only provide clarity to your collection but will also make your journey more personally meaningful.

2. **Educate Yourself:** Knowledge is the cornerstone of successful coin collecting. Take the time to educate yourself about different types of coins, grading systems, and historical contexts. Books, online resources, and engaging with experienced collectors can enhance your understanding of numismatics. The greater your knowledge, the more prepared you'll be to make well-informed choices regarding your collection.

3. **Set Realistic Objectives:** Establish both short-term and long-term goals for your coin collection. Short-term goals might involve acquiring specific coins or completing a set, while long-term goals could include building a comprehensive collection from a particular era or achieving expertise in a specialized area of numismatics. Ensure that your goals are

realistic, considering factors such as budget, availability, and your personal level of commitment to the hobby.

4. **Budget Wisely:** Numismatics can be as affordable or as expensive as you make it. Before diving into collecting, establish a realistic budget that aligns with your financial situation. Consider factors such as the rarity of coins you're interested in, their condition, and the potential for future investments. Being mindful of your budget ensures that your numismatic pursuits remain enjoyable and sustainable.

5. **Network and Engage:** Coin collecting is a social hobby. Connect with other collectors, both online and in person. Join numismatic forums, attend coin shows, and participate in local collector groups. Networking with fellow enthusiasts not only provides valuable insights but also opens up opportunities for trading, learning, and expanding your collection. The collective knowledge within the numismatic community can be an invaluable resource as you navigate your coin collecting journey.

6. **Preservation and Display:** Consider how you want to store and display your collection. Proper preservation is essential for maintaining the condition and value of your coins. Options range from protective holders and albums to display cases and cabinets. Choosing the right storage methods not only safeguards your coins but also enhances the visual appeal of your collection. Organizing and showcasing your coins adds a personal touch to your numismatic experience.

7. **Document Your Journey:** Keep a comprehensive record of your collection. Create a catalog detailing the history and significance of each coin. This documentation functions as a valuable resource for enhancing your own understanding and can also be shared with fellow collectors. Whether you favor a tangible notebook or a digital database, keeping a record of your journey adds a meaningful dimension to your numismatic endeavors.

8. **Adapt and Evolve:** Numismatics is a dynamic hobby. As you delve deeper into collecting, be open to adapting your goals and expanding your collection. New discoveries, changing interests, and unforeseen opportunities may influence the trajectory of your numismatic journey. Embrace the evolution of your collection as part of the ongoing joy of coin collecting.

9. **Attend Coin Shows and Events:** Try to attend coin shows and numismatic events. These gatherings provide a unique opportunity to view a wide variety of coins, engage with dealers and other collectors, and stay updated on the latest trends in the numismatic world. Coin shows can be not only educational but also inspirational, fueling your passion for collecting.

10. **Contribute to the Community:** Consider contributing to the numismatic community. Share your knowledge, experiences, and insights with fellow collectors. This can be done through online forums, articles, or even organizing local coin-related events. Contributing to the community not only enhances your own understanding of numismatics but also fosters a sense of camaraderie within the collector community.

As you venture into the enchanting world of coin collecting, remember that each coin in your collection is not just a piece of metal but a tangible link to the diverse and fascinating chapters of human history. Enjoy the thrill of the hunt, the joy of discovery, and the camaraderie of fellow collectors as you build a collection that reflects both your personal passions and the timeless allure of numismatics. May your numismatic journey be as rewarding as the treasures you uncover along the way.

Chapter 2:

Getting Started

Embarking on the journey of coin collecting is a thrilling endeavor that promises a rich tapestry of history, art, and personal discovery. In this chapter, we'll guide you through the foundational steps of getting started in numismatics. From building your numismatic knowledge to assembling your coin collecting toolkit, each element contributes to a well-rounded and enjoyable experience in the fascinating world of coin collecting.

Building Your Numismatic Knowledge

Understanding the coins you collect is fundamental to the depth and richness of your numismatic journey. A solid foundation of knowledge allows you to appreciate the historical context, artistic nuances, and cultural significance of each coin in your collection. Here are key aspects to consider as you build your numismatic knowledge:

1. **Historical Context**

Immerse yourself in the historical context of the coins you collect. Each coin is a small but significant artifact that reflects the era in which it was minted. Take the U.S. Morgan Silver Dollar, for example. Minted from 1878 to 1921, the Morgan Dollar carries the legacy of the Wild West, the Industrial Revolution, and the economic transformations of the late nineteenth and early twentieth centuries. Understanding the historical backdrop allows you to appreciate the role these coins played in shaping the narrative of their time.

Similarly, the U.S. Liberty Head Nickel, minted from 1883 to 1913, is a testament to the optimism and innovation of the Gilded Age. Its iconic design featuring Lady Liberty and the majestic buffalo on the reverse captures the spirit of a nation expanding westward. The Liberty Head Nickel provides a visual snapshot of an era marked by progress and change.

2. Artistic Styles

Coins serve as miniature canvases for artistic expression. Explore the artistic styles represented in different coins to gain a deeper understanding of their visual language. The U.S. Indian Head Penny, struck from 1859 to 1909, is a prime example of numismatic artistry. Designed by James B. Longacre, the coin features a profile of Lady Liberty adorned with a Native American headdress. The complex details of the design highlight the fusion of classical and indigenous elements, making it a captivating piece of art.

The U.S. Buffalo Nickel, minted from 1913 to 1938, is another masterpiece of numismatic design. Sculptor James Earle Fraser's depiction of a Native American and a buffalo on the coin's obverse and reverse, respectively, showcases a harmonious blend of realism and symbolism. Understanding the artistic nuances of these coins elevates your appreciation for the craftsmanship and creativity that went into their creation.

3. Grading

Grading is a critical aspect of numismatics that involves evaluating the condition of a coin. Familiarize yourself with grading systems to accurately assess the quality of your coins. The U.S. Lincoln Wheat Penny, struck from 1909 to 1958, provides an excellent case study in grading. Differentiating between coins in circulated condition and those in mint state can significantly impact their value. Learning the intricacies of grading allows you to identify coins with exceptional preservation and, in turn, make informed decisions in your collecting journey.

4. Diversification of Knowledge

While it's natural to have specific interests, diversifying your knowledge adds depth to your numismatic expertise. Explore coins from different regions, time periods, and cultures to broaden your understanding. While focusing on U.S. coins, consider venturing into international numismatics to appreciate the global scope of coinage. A well-rounded collector is not only more informed but also better equipped to navigate the diverse landscape of numismatics.

For instance, studying the U.S. Liberty Head Nickel alongside its Canadian counterpart, the Canadian Liberty Head Nickel, provides insights into the shared history and artistic influences between neighboring nations. Comparing and contrasting coins from different regions enhances your ability to recognize unique features and appreciate the diversity within the numismatic world.

5. Utilization of Resources

Take advantage of the wealth of resources available to coin collectors. Books, online articles, forums, and reputable websites serve as valuable references. The U.S. Buffalo Nickel, with its various minting varieties and historical significance, has been extensively documented in numismatic literature. Accessing resources specific to this coin, such as the works of renowned numismatists, can deepen your understanding and aid in the identification of key attributes.

Numismatic organizations, such as the American Numismatic Association (ANA), provide access to educational materials, events, and knowledgeable experts. Online forums and social media groups dedicated to specific coins, such as the U.S. Morgan Silver Dollar, offer platforms for discussions, sharing experiences, and seeking advice from fellow collectors.

6. Engagement with Experienced Collectors

Connecting with experienced collectors is a valuable aspect of building your numismatic knowledge. Engage with seasoned collectors who can offer insights, share their experiences, and provide guidance on specific coins. Numismatic clubs and local meet-ups offer opportunities to interact with enthusiasts who may have specialized knowledge in areas like U.S. Indian Head Pennies or Liberty Nickels. Learning from those with hands-on experience enriches your own collecting journey.

Establishing mentorship relationships with experienced collectors can be particularly beneficial. Mentors can provide personalized guidance, share their expertise, and introduce you to advanced aspects of numismatics. Whether through in-person meetings or online communities, the shared passion for coins fosters a sense of camaraderie that contributes to the overall enjoyment of the hobby.

7. Visits to Museums and Exhibitions

Museums and coin exhibitions provide a unique opportunity to view rare and historically significant coins in person. Take the time to explore exhibits featuring coins like the U.S. Morgan Silver Dollar in a curated setting. Viewing coins in a museum context allows you to appreciate the details, craftsmanship, and historical context in a way that photographs or descriptions alone cannot capture.

Many museums organize special exhibitions focused on specific coins or periods, providing a deeper dive into the stories behind the coins. Participating in guided tours or educational programs enhances your understanding and offers a more immersive experience. Museums often collaborate with numismatic experts, creating a valuable synergy between institutional knowledge and individual collectors.

8. Staying Curious

Numismatics is a dynamic field that continually evolves. Cultivate a curious mindset and remain open to learning. Attend lectures, webinars, and other educational events to stay informed about the latest developments in numismatics. Subscribe to newsletters and publications that provide updates on new discoveries, research findings, and upcoming coin releases.

Applying curiosity to your collecting journey encourages exploration beyond familiar territories. Investigate lesser-known coins or delve into the historical context of specific minting years. Staying curious ensures that your numismatic knowledge remains vibrant and relevant in the ever-changing landscape of coin collecting.

Assembling Your Coin Collecting Toolkit

Equipping yourself with the right tools is essential for a fulfilling and successful coin collecting journey. Your toolkit not only enhances your ability to assess, preserve, and enjoy your coins but also ensures that you are well-prepared to navigate the diverse world of numismatics. In this section, we will explore the comprehensive elements of assembling your coin collecting toolkit, providing insights into the essential tools and resources that every collector should consider.

1. **Magnification Tools:** Magnification tools are fundamental for closely examining the details of your coins. A good-quality magnifying glass or a jeweler's loupe allows you to scrutinize mint marks, detect wear, and appreciate the fine nuances of coin designs. Opt for tools with sufficient magnification and clarity to ensure a detailed examination of your collection.

2. **Gloves:** Handling coins with bare hands can transfer oils and contaminants, potentially affecting their condition. Invest in cotton or nitrile gloves to ensure that you handle your coins with care. Wearing gloves minimizes the risk of leaving fingerprints and helps preserve the pristine state of your coins, particularly for those in uncirculated or proof condition.

3. **Digital Scale:** A digital scale is a valuable tool for accurately measuring the weight of coins. Weight can be a crucial factor in identifying counterfeit coins or determining the authenticity of a particular issue. Choose a scale with a high level of precision for accurate measurements, especially if you are dealing with coins where weight discrepancies can be significant.

4. **Calipers:** Calipers are useful for measuring the diameter and thickness of coins. These measurements can provide additional information about a coin's authenticity and aid in determining its grade. Digital calipers offer precision and ease of use, allowing you to make accurate assessments of your coins' physical attributes.

5. **Coin Holders and Capsules:** Proper storage is paramount for preserving the condition of your coins. Invest in high-quality coin holders, capsules, or holders made of materials that are free from PVC and other harmful substances. These protective enclosures safeguard coins from environmental elements and physical damage. Choose holders that fit your coins securely to prevent movement and potential scratching.

6. **Albums and Folders:** Organizing your collection is made easier with the use of albums and folders. These tools provide a systematic way to display and store your coins, allowing you to track your progress in completing sets and showcasing your collection to others. Consider archival-quality albums and folders to ensure the long-term preservation of your coins.

7. **Cleaning Supplies:** While cleaning coins is generally discouraged, having mild cleaning supplies, such as distilled water and a soft brush, can be useful for removing surface dirt. However, it's crucial to exercise extreme caution to avoid damaging the coin's patina or historical integrity. If cleaning is necessary, consult reputable sources for guidance on appropriate methods and materials.

8. **Reference Books:** A collection of reference books tailored to your specific interests is an invaluable resource. Whether focused on ancient coins, U.S. coinage, or world coins, reference books provide detailed information, historical context, and pricing guides to aid

in your collecting journey. Regularly update your library to stay informed about new discoveries and research findings in the numismatic field.

9. **Storage Solutions:** Consider the long-term storage of your collection. Safes or safety deposit boxes provide secure environments for valuable coins. Additionally, investing in climate-controlled storage helps prevent environmental factors, such as humidity, from affecting the condition of your coins. Evaluate your storage needs based on the size and value of your collection, ensuring that each coin is protected for future generations.

10. **Digital Camera:** Documenting your collection is essential for both personal enjoyment and potential future appraisal. A digital camera with macro capabilities allows you to capture high-quality images of your coins, preserving their details and serving as a visual record of your numismatic journey. Regularly photograph your coins, especially if you make additions to your collection, to maintain a comprehensive digital archive.

11. **Numismatic Software or Cataloging Tools:** Utilize numismatic software or cataloging tools to maintain a detailed inventory of your collection. These tools often include features such as grading assistance, pricing databases, and organizational options, streamlining the management of your growing collection. Choose software that aligns with your collecting goals and preferences, making it easier to track acquisitions, sales, and changes in coin values.

12. **Security Measures:** Implement security measures to safeguard your collection. Consider installing a home security system or utilizing a safe deposit box for high-value coins. Keep detailed records of your collection, including photographs, descriptions, and any relevant appraisals. Being proactive about security ensures the protection of your investment and the preservation of your numismatic legacy.

Example Coins:

1. **Medieval Gold Florin**

When examining intricate details on a Medieval Gold Florin, a high-quality magnifying glass or jeweler's loupe is indispensable. These tools allow you to appreciate the fine craftsmanship and detect any subtle wear or mint marks.

2. **Spanish Doubloon**

Handling a valuable coin like the Spanish Doubloon requires the use of gloves to prevent the transfer of oils and contaminants. Additionally, a digital scale becomes crucial for accurately measuring the weight of the Doubloon, aiding in authentication.

3. Spanish 8 Reales Coin (Pieces of Eight)

For a coin with historical significance like the Spanish 8 Reales (Pieces of Eight), reference books play a vital role. They provide detailed information on the coin's historical context, aiding collectors in understanding its importance in the numismatic world.

These examples illustrate how specific tools in your coin collecting toolkit cater to the unique characteristics and needs of different coins in your collection.

Chapter 3:

Identifying Coins

Identifying coins is a foundational skill for every coin collector. It not only enhances your appreciation for the vast diversity within numismatics but also plays a crucial role in assessing the rarity and value of your collection. This chapter delves into the intricacies of coin identification, offering insights into understanding various coin types and the art of discerning their unique varieties.

Coin Types and Varieties

Numismatics encompasses a vast array of coin types and varieties, each with its unique characteristics, historical significance, and collector appeal. In this section, we will delve into a diverse spectrum of coin types, from gold and silver coins to commemorative coins, ancient coins, and beyond. Understanding the nuances of each coin type enriches your numismatic knowledge and broadens the horizons of your collecting journey.

Gold and Silver Coins

- **Gold Coins**

Gold coins have captivated collectors for centuries, symbolizing wealth, prestige, and artistic excellence. From ancient civilizations to modern mintings, gold coins come in various denominations and designs. Iconic examples include the U.S. Double Eagle, the British Sovereign, and the South African Krugerrand. Gold coins are often prized not only for their precious metal content but also for their historical and aesthetic appeal.

- **Silver Coins**

Silver coins, like gold, hold a prominent place in numismatic history. The lustrous beauty of silver, coupled with its more accessible nature compared to gold, makes silver coins widely collected. Examples include the U.S. Morgan Silver Dollar, the Canadian Silver Maple Leaf, and the Mexican Silver Libertad. Silver coins often showcase intricate designs and offer collectors the opportunity to explore a diverse range of themes and artistic styles.

Commemorative Coins

Commemorative coins are issued to mark and celebrate specific events, anniversaries, or individuals. These coins go beyond the regular circulation issues and are often crafted with special designs and limited mintages. Collectors are drawn to commemoratives for their historical significance and unique artistic expressions. Notable examples include the U.S. Silver Commemorative Half Dollars, which honor events like the Columbian Exposition and the Statue of Liberty centennial.

Revolutionary Coins

Coins minted during revolutionary periods hold a special place in numismatic history. These coins often bear symbols of political change, national identity, and the aspirations of a people seeking independence. Examples include the French Revolutionary Assignats and the American Colonial and Continental Currency issues. Revolutionary coins serve as tangible links to moments of societal transformation and are highly sought after by collectors interested in political and historical numismatics.

Ancient Coins

Ancient coins transport collectors back in time, offering glimpses into the civilizations that once thrived. Greek, Roman, Byzantine, and Egyptian coins, among others, showcase the art, culture, and political ideologies of their respective eras. Each coin tells a story, whether it's a silver tetradrachm from ancient Greece or a denarius from the Roman Empire. Collectors of ancient coins engage in a fascinating journey of discovery, unraveling the mysteries of the past through these small, enduring artifacts.

Souvenir Coins

Souvenir coins, often associated with tourist destinations or special events, serve as tangible mementos. These coins may feature iconic landmarks, cultural symbols, or historical references related to a specific location. Collectors who appreciate the intersection of numismatics and travel find joy in assembling souvenir coin collections that reflect their explorations and experiences.

Medallions

While not legal tender, medallions are often included in numismatic collections due to their artistic merit and historical themes. Medallions are larger and thicker than traditional coins and are crafted for commemorative purposes. They may depict famous figures, events, or artistic representations. Medallions offer collectors an opportunity to appreciate numismatic artistry beyond the constraints of circulating currency.

Tokens

Tokens, unlike coins, are not issued by governments but are instead created by private entities for specific purposes. They can represent various themes, including transportation, trade, or advertising. Collectors of tokens appreciate the historical and regional diversity these items bring to a collection. Examples include transit tokens, trade tokens, and arcade tokens.

Error Coins

Error coins are minted with mistakes or abnormalities, making them unique and intriguing to collectors. These errors can include off-center strikes, double strikes, planchet errors, and more. Collectors of error coins are drawn to the rarity and uniqueness of these specimens, as they often represent unintended variations in the minting process.

BU Rolls

Brilliant Uncirculated (BU) rolls consist of coins that have never been in circulation and exhibit a high level of detail and luster. Collectors often seek BU rolls to obtain pristine examples of coins for their collections. These rolls can include coins from various denominations and mint years, providing a comprehensive snapshot of a specific issue in its original, untouched condition.

Silver Certificates

Silver certificates are a form of paper currency issued by the U.S. government that could be exchanged for a specific amount of silver. Though no longer in circulation, silver certificates are collected for their historical significance and unique designs. Collectors often seek examples that showcase different silver certificate series and signatures.

Art Bars

Art bars are silver bars that feature artistic designs, often produced by private mints or refineries. These bars go beyond the traditional concept of bullion and serve as collectible pieces of art. Art bar collectors appreciate the combination of precious metal investment and artistic expression, with each bar often showcasing unique themes, designs, or historical motifs.

Bullion Coins

Bullion coins are minted primarily for their precious metal content and are often sought after by investors for their intrinsic value. Examples comprise the American Gold Eagle, Canadian Maple

Leaf, and South African Krugerrand. While investors focus on the metal content, numismatic collectors appreciate the beauty and craftsmanship of these coins, often building collections based on specific series or themes.

Building Your Collection with Intention
As a collector, the diverse array of coin types and varieties provides endless opportunities to build a collection with intention and personal meaning. Whether you are drawn to the historical depth of ancient coins, the artistry of commemorative issues, or the tangible connections offered by revolutionary coins, each category contributes to the rich tapestry of numismatics.

Consider defining the focus of your collection based on your interests, whether they lie in a specific time period, geographical region, or thematic element. Some collectors may choose to specialize in a single category, such as ancient Roman coins, while others embrace a more eclectic approach, assembling a collection that spans various types and periods.

Numismatic knowledge plays a crucial role in guiding your collecting journey. Research and education empower you to make informed decisions, identify valuable specimens, and appreciate the historical and artistic significance of the coins you acquire. As you explore the diverse world of coin types and varieties, remember that the joy of collecting lies not only in the coins themselves but in the stories they tell and the connections they forge across time and cultures.

Strategies for Building a Diverse Collection

4. **Thematic Collections:** Organize your collection around specific themes that resonate with your interests. Whether it's a focus on animals, historical figures, or events, a thematic approach adds coherence and personal significance to your collection.

5. **Period-Based Collections:** Build collections centered around specific historical periods, such as ancient civilizations, medieval coinage, or modern eras. This approach allows you to explore the evolution of coinage over time and delve into the historical context of each period.

6. **Geographical Collections:** Explore coins from different regions and countries to appreciate the diversity of numismatics. Building collections based on geographical locations provides insights into the cultural and economic factors that influenced coin designs and minting practices.

7. **Material-Centric Collections:** Focus on collections centered around specific materials, such as gold or silver coins. This approach allows you to explore the unique qualities and characteristics of each metal, as well as the historical significance attached to them.

8. **Mintmark Collections:** Collect coins based on mintmarks, exploring the variations and minting practices of different mints. Mintmark collections can include coins from various periods and regions, offering a comprehensive view of minting history.

9. **Error Coin Collections:** Embrace the uniqueness of error coins by building a collection that highlights minting mistakes and abnormalities. Error coins add an element of surprise and rarity to your collection, making each specimen distinctive.

10. **Circulation and Currency Collections:** Assemble collections that focus on coins that circulated in everyday commerce. This approach provides a tangible connection to the economic history of different periods and regions, showcasing the coins that were once used in daily transactions.

11. **Investment-Grade Collections:** For collectors who also view their collections as investments, focusing on high-grade or rare coins can be a strategy. These collections may include coins with significant numismatic value or those with potential for future appreciation.

The Art of Coin Identification

Coin identification serves as the foundation of a collector's knowledge. It involves the recognition of key attributes, such as design elements, mint marks, dates, and denominations, which collectively define a coin. Accurate identification is crucial for assessing a coin's rarity, historical significance, and market value. Additionally, it contributes to the organization and categorization of a collection, allowing collectors to create cohesive and well-documented sets.

The Anatomy of Coin Identification

- **Obverse and Reverse**

The obverse and reverse of a coin refer to its front and back, respectively. The obverse typically features a portrait, symbol, or image representing the issuing authority, while the reverse showcases various designs, such as national emblems, animals, or commemorative themes. The identification process often begins by examining these two sides to determine the coin's country of origin and denomination.

- **Design Elements**

The design elements of a coin include images, inscriptions, and motifs that convey artistic and historical meaning. Analyzing these elements is crucial for identifying specific coin types. For example, the U.S. Walking Liberty Half Dollar is known for its elegant depiction of Liberty walking and the U.S. flag, while the U.S. Franklin Half Dollar features a portrait of Benjamin Franklin.

- **Date and Mint Mark**

The date and mint mark provide essential information for identifying and cataloging coins. The date indicates the year of minting, while the mint mark signifies the location where the coin was minted. For U.S. coins, mint marks include letters such as "D" for Denver and "S" for San Francisco. The location and size of these marks vary depending on the coin.

- **Denomination**

The denomination of a coin refers to its face value, such as one cent, five cents, or one dollar. Understanding denominations is fundamental for coin identification, as it helps collectors categorize coins within their collections and differentiate between various issues.

- **Edge Design**

Some coins feature unique edge designs that aid in identification. Reeded edges, smooth edges, and lettered edges are among the variations. Examining the edge design becomes particularly relevant when identifying coins that share similar obverse and reverse features.

U.S. Walking Liberty Half Dollar

The U.S. Walking Liberty Half Dollar, minted from 1916 to 1947, is renowned for its iconic design by Adolph A. Weinman. The obverse features a graceful Lady Liberty walking toward the sun, symbolizing freedom and optimism. The reverse displays an eagle perched on a mountain ledge, evoking a sense of strength and majesty. To identify a Walking Liberty Half Dollar, look for the walking Liberty figure, the date on the obverse, and the mint mark on the reverse.

U.S. Franklin Half Dollar

The U.S. Franklin Half Dollar, minted from 1948 to 1963, bears the portrait of one of America's founding fathers, Benjamin Franklin. The obverse features Franklin's profile, while the reverse displays the Liberty Bell. To identify a Franklin Half Dollar, focus on Franklin's distinctive image, the date, and the mint mark, usually found on the reverse above the Liberty Bell.

U.S. Kennedy Half Dollar

The U.S. Kennedy Half Dollar, introduced in 1964, was minted to honor President John F. Kennedy following his assassination. The obverse features a profile of Kennedy, while the reverse displays the presidential seal. Identifying a Kennedy Half Dollar involves recognizing Kennedy's image, the date, and the mint mark, typically found on the reverse.

U.S. Eisenhower Dollar

The U.S. Eisenhower Dollar, minted from 1971 to 1978, commemorates President Dwight D. Eisenhower. The obverse features Eisenhower's profile, while the reverse displays an eagle landing on the moon, representing the Apollo 11 mission. Identifying an Eisenhower Dollar entails recognizing Eisenhower's image, the date, and the mint mark, typically located on the obverse.

U.S. Silver Eagle

The U.S. Silver Eagle, first minted in 1986, is a bullion coin known for its silver content and striking design. The obverse features Adolph A. Weinman's Walking Liberty design, while the reverse displays John Mercanti's heraldic eagle. Identifying a Silver Eagle involves recognizing these iconic designs, the date, and any mint marks.

Advanced Identification Techniques

1. **Die Varieties:** Die varieties occur when different dies are used in the minting process, resulting in subtle differences in design elements. Identifying die varieties requires a keen eye and often involves close examination of specific details, such as doubling on lettering or distinct features on the coin.

2. **Overdates and Repunched Mint Marks:** Overdates occur when a coin is struck with a die that bears a date from a previous year. Repunched mint marks happen when the mint mark is stamped multiple times. Identifying these nuances requires careful scrutiny and familiarity with minting variations.

3. **Counterstamps and Countermarks:** Counterstamps and countermarks involve adding additional marks to a coin after it has been minted. These marks can indicate historical events, counterfeiting attempts, or special issuances. Identifying counterstamps requires research into the specific markings and their significance.

4. **Diagnostic Features:** Some coins have diagnostic features that aid in identification, such as unique die cracks, misplaced mint marks, or distinct luster patterns. These features often require a combination of visual inspection and, in some cases, specialized tools.

The art of coin identification is a continuous journey of learning and discovery. As you delve into the details of each coin, you not only enhance your ability to recognize and categorize them but also deepen your appreciation for the historical, artistic, and technical aspects of numismatics.

Engage with the numismatic community, attend events, and embrace the wealth of resources available to collectors. The coins you identify become more than mere artifacts; they become portals to history, storytelling devices that connect you to the past.

Chapter 4:

Valuing Your Collection

As a passionate numismatist, the value of your coin collection extends beyond its monetary worth. While the thrill of discovery, historical narratives, and aesthetic appreciation are priceless aspects of collecting, understanding the monetary value of your coins adds a practical dimension to your numismatic journey.

Factors Affecting Coin Value

The value of a coin in the world of numismatics is a multifaceted concept, influenced by a myriad of factors that contribute to its overall worth. Whether you're a seasoned collector or a newcomer to the hobby, understanding these factors is essential for navigating the intricate landscape of coin valuation. In this comprehensive exploration, we will delve into the key elements that affect the value of a coin, shaping its desirability and market appeal.

1. **Rarity**

Rarity stands as one of the fundamental pillars of coin value. In the numismatic realm, scarcity enhances desirability. Coins with low mintages, limited surviving specimens, or those featuring unique variations become prized possessions among collectors. Rarity is not only about the total number of coins minted but also about the number of coins available in the desired condition. A coin might be common overall but rare in higher grades, elevating its value due to condition rarity.

Example: U.S. State Quarters

The U.S. State Quarters program, launched in 1999, featured a series of quarters representing each state in the order of its admission to the Union. While the mintages of these quarters were generally high, certain error coins, such as the Wisconsin Extra Leaf variety, are considered rare and highly sought after by collectors.

2. Condition (Grading)

The condition or grade of a coin is a critical determinant of its value. Grading, a standardized system of evaluating a coin's state of preservation, considers factors such as wear, surface quality, and overall appeal. Coins in higher grades, such as Mint State or Proof, command higher prices in the market. The grading process, conducted by professional grading services like the NGC or the PCGS, provides a universally recognized assessment that influences a coin's perceived value.

Example: British Gold Sovereign

Consider the British Gold Sovereign, a coin with historical significance and a rich legacy. A Gold Sovereign in Mint State (MS) condition, indicating a well-preserved and uncirculated state, is likely to fetch a higher value compared to a similar coin with signs of wear and circulation.

3. Historical Significance

Coins with historical significance often carry additional value. Whether tied to pivotal events, notable figures, or specific periods, the historical context enriches the narrative of a coin. Collectors are drawn to coins that bear witness to significant moments in history, appreciating them not only as artifacts but as tangible links to the past.

Example: U.S. Commemorative Coins

U.S. Commemorative Coins are issued to mark significant events or honor notable figures. For instance, the 1921 Alabama Centennial Half Dollar, commemorating the 100th anniversary of Alabama's admission to the Union, holds historical significance. Collectors seeking coins tied to specific historical events may find added value in such commemoratives.

4. Numismatic Rarity and Popularity

Numismatic rarity and popularity contribute to a coin's value. Some coins gain prominence over time, becoming sought after by collectors due to their significance within a specific series, design type, or historical era. Popularity can be influenced by cultural trends, renewed interest in certain themes, or even by the appeal of a particular coin design.

Example: British Shilling

The British Shilling, with its long history dating back to the Anglo-Saxon period, has numismatic significance. Older shillings from specific reigns, such as those of Queen Elizabeth I, are popular among collectors seeking coins with both historical and numismatic value.

5. Demand and Market Trends

The basic economic principle of supply and demand plays a pivotal role in determining coin values. Coins experiencing high demand due to collector interest or market trends may see an increase in value. Conversely, coins facing decreased demand may experience price fluctuations. Staying attuned to market trends helps collectors make informed decisions regarding the buying, selling, and holding of their coins.

6. Metal Content

For coins with intrinsic value derived from precious metals like gold, silver, or platinum, the market prices of these metals directly impact the coin's value. The metal content provides a baseline value, often referred to as the bullion value. Understanding the current market prices of precious metals is crucial for accurately assessing the worth of bullion and precious metal coins.

7. Cultural or Artistic Significance

Coins that possess cultural or artistic significance often command higher values. Whether it's an intricately designed commemorative coin or a coin showcasing exceptional craftsmanship, the artistic appeal contributes to its desirability. Artistic elements can include unique designs, skilled engraving, or representations of cultural symbols, enhancing the coin's aesthetic appeal and collector interest.

8. Provenance

The provenance, or documented history of ownership, can influence a coin's value. Coins with notable provenance, such as those once part of famous collections or with well-documented pedigrees, may carry additional worth. The provenance provides a sense of authenticity and a connection to previous owners, adding a layer of historical context to the coin.

9. Condition Rarity

Condition rarity refers to coins that are rare in high grades. A coin may be relatively common overall, but finding it in top-tier conditions can be a challenging task. Collectors often seek out condition rarities, and these coins may command higher prices due to their exceptional state of preservation.

10. Crossover Collectibility

Coins with crossover collectibility appeal to a broader audience, transcending specific niches within numismatics. These coins attract collectors with varied interests, combining elements of historical significance, artistic appeal, or thematic relevance. Crossover collectibles often experience increased demand, influencing their market values.

11. Varieties and Errors

Coins with unique varieties or errors often carry increased value. Collectors are drawn to the distinctiveness of these coins, whether it's a doubled die, off-center strike, or other unusual characteristics. Varieties and errors add an element of intrigue and uniqueness to a coin, making them highly sought after in the numismatic community.

Understanding these factors is crucial for collectors seeking to assess the value of their coins accurately. While each factor contributes to a coin's overall worth, the interplay of these elements creates a dynamic and ever-evolving landscape within the numismatic market.

Appraisal and Valuation Methods

Appraising and valuing a coin collection is both an art and a science, requiring a nuanced understanding of numismatics, market dynamics, and the specific attributes that contribute to a coin's worth. In this section, we will delve into the various methods employed by collectors and professionals to appraise and value coins, providing insights into the intricacies of determining the monetary value of numismatic treasures.

1. Professional Appraisal Services

One of the most reliable methods for determining the value of a coin collection is through professional appraisal services. Numismatic experts, often affiliated with reputable coin dealerships or independent appraisal firms, possess the expertise to thoroughly evaluate individual coins and entire collections. Professional appraisers consider factors like rarity, historical significance, condition, and market demand in their assessments.

Advantages:

- **Expertise:** Professional appraisers bring a wealth of knowledge and experience to the evaluation process.
- **Accuracy:** Their expertise allows for a precise and accurate appraisal, considering both the individual attributes of coins and broader market trends.
- **Documentation:** Appraisal reports generated by professionals serve as valuable documentation for insurance purposes, estate planning, and future sales.

Considerations:

- **Cost:** Professional appraisals may come with associated fees, but the accuracy and reliability often justify the expense.
- **Choosing the Right Appraiser:** It's crucial to select a reputable and experienced appraiser with a background in numismatics.

2. Grading Services

Numismatic grading services, like the NGC and the PCGS, play a significant role in determining a coin's value. These services use standardized grading scales to assess a coin's condition, providing a clear and universally recognized measure of its state of preservation.

Advantages:

- **Uniformity:** Grading services offer a standardized and consistent approach to evaluating coins, ensuring that collectors, dealers, and investors have a common understanding of a coin's condition.
- **Market Acceptance:** Graded coins often enjoy higher market acceptance and may command premium prices due to the assurance of their graded state.
- **Protection:** Coins encapsulated in tamper-evident holders by grading services are protected from environmental factors, preserving their condition.

Considerations:

- **Cost:** Grading services typically involve fees for each coin submitted. Collectors should weigh the benefits against the associated costs.
- **Authentication:** While grading services primarily focus on condition, they also provide authentication, ensuring that the coin is genuine.

3. Auction Houses

Auction houses are integral to the coin market, offering a platform for buying and selling rare and valuable coins. Consigning your collection to a reputable auction house allows your coins to be presented to a wide audience of collectors, potentially leading to competitive bidding and fair market values.

Advantages:

- **Market Exposure:** Auction houses provide extensive market exposure, attracting serious collectors and investors.
- **Competitive Bidding:** The auction format often results in competitive bidding, maximizing the potential value of your coins.
- **Professional Marketing:** Auction houses employ professional marketing strategies to promote upcoming auctions, creating anticipation and interest in featured coins.

Considerations:

- **Seller's Fees:** Auction houses typically charge seller's fees, which are a percentage of the final sale price. Sellers should factor these fees into their considerations.
- **Timing:** Choosing the right auction and timing can significantly impact the success of the sale.

4. **Online Platforms and Marketplaces**

In the era of digitalization, online markets and platforms have become vital channels for buying, selling, and valuing coins. Websites, forums, and auction platforms cater to a global audience of collectors and investors, providing a convenient and accessible way to assess market values.

Advantages:

- **Global Reach:** Online platforms offer access to a global community of collectors and buyers, expanding the potential market for your coins.
- **Transparency:** Completed sales, auction results, and ongoing market trends are often accessible online, providing valuable insights for valuation.
- **Ease of Transactions:** Online transactions are convenient and may involve lower transaction costs compared to traditional methods.

Considerations:

- **Authentication and Verification:** Due diligence is crucial when transacting online. Ensure the authenticity of the platform and the identity of the parties involved.
- **Condition Disclosure:** Clearly communicate the condition of your coins through detailed descriptions and high-quality images.

5. **Price Guides and Catalogs**

Numismatic price guides and catalogs, such as the Red Book for U.S. coins, serve as valuable reference tools for collectors seeking to assess the value of their coins. These publications provide historical pricing data, mintage figures, and insights into market trends.

Advantages:

- **Reference Points:** Price guides offer reference points for assessing the value of coins based on historical pricing data.
- **Educational Resource:** Collectors can gain insights into mintage figures, key attributes, and historical context through these guides.
- **Informed Decision-Making:** Price guides help collectors make informed decisions about buying, selling, or holding coins in their collection.

Considerations:

- **Dynamic Market:** Market values are dynamic, and price guides may not capture real-time fluctuations. It's essential to supplement guide information with current market research.

6. Comparative Sales Analysis

Conducting a comparative analysis involves researching recent sales of similar coins to assess their market values. This method relies on examining comparable coins with similar attributes, such as date, mint mark, and condition.

Advantages:

- **Real-Time Insights:** Comparative sales analysis provides real-time insights into the current market values of coins similar to those in your collection.
- **Specific Attribute Focus:** This method allows collectors to focus on coins with similar attributes, providing a more targeted approach to valuation.

Considerations:

- **Market Variability:** Market values can vary, and trends may change. Regular updates and ongoing research are necessary for accurate comparative analysis.
- **Data Credibility:** Ensure that the data used for comparison is from credible sources and reflects recent transactions.

7. Networking with Collectors

Engaging with fellow collectors and numismatic communities offers a qualitative method of assessing coin values. Discussions with experienced collectors provide valuable insights into market trends, current demands, and the specific attributes that collectors find appealing.

Advantages:

- **Community Insights:** Networking with collectors allows you to tap into the collective knowledge and insights of the numismatic community.
- **Experiential Knowledge:** Experienced collectors can share their experiences with similar coins, shedding light on potential market values.
- **Personalized Advice:** The personal touch of networking allows for personalized advice tailored to your specific collection.

Considerations:

- **Diverse Perspectives:** While networking provides valuable insights, opinions may vary. Consider gathering input from multiple sources for a well-rounded perspective.
- **Stay Informed:** Actively participate in collector communities to stay informed about the latest market trends and developments.

8. **Numismatic Events and Shows**

Numismatic events, coin shows, and conventions provide collectors with opportunities to showcase their collections, receive expert opinions, and gauge market interest. These events offer a hands-on experience and a chance to connect with dealers and fellow enthusiasts.

Advantages:

- **Expert Consultation:** Numismatic events often feature expert consultations, allowing collectors to receive professional opinions on their collections.
- **Potential Sales:** Coin shows may attract potential buyers, providing opportunities for sales and trades.
- **Hands-On Evaluation:** Collectors can physically examine coins and discuss their collections with experts, adding a tangible dimension to the appraisal process.

Considerations:

- **Event Participation Costs:** Participation in events may involve costs such as booth fees or registration fees. Evaluate the potential benefits against these costs.
- **Timing and Planning:** Choosing the right events and planning effectively contribute to the success of your participation.

9. **Metal Content Valuation**

For coins with significant precious metal content, the valuation can be calculated based on the current market prices of the metals involved. This method is particularly relevant for bullion coins, which derive a substantial portion of their value from the intrinsic worth of the metals.

Advantages:

- **Intrinsic Value Calculation:** Metal content valuation provides a straightforward method for determining the intrinsic value of bullion and precious metal coins.
- **Market-Driven:** The valuation aligns with current market prices of precious metals, offering a real-time assessment.

Considerations:

- **Metal Price Volatility:** Precious metal prices can be volatile. Regularly monitor market fluctuations for accurate valuations.
- **Numismatic Premium:** Consider that bullion coins often carry a numismatic premium in addition to their metal content value.

10. Multiple Appraisal Opinions

Seeking multiple appraisal opinions can provide a more comprehensive understanding of your collection's value. Different appraisers may offer varying perspectives, helping you establish a well-rounded valuation that considers various factors.

Advantages:

- **Diverse Perspectives:** Multiple appraisals provide diverse perspectives, enhancing your understanding of the market and the potential value of your collection.
- **Verification of Assessments:** Consistent assessments across multiple appraisers can validate the accuracy of the appraisals.
- **Negotiation Leverage:** Having multiple appraisals can provide leverage in negotiations, especially when considering sales or trades.

Considerations:

- **Appraiser Credibility:** Ensure that all appraisers consulted are reputable, experienced, and have a background in numismatics.
- **Objective Comparisons:** Evaluate the appraisals objectively, considering the methodologies used and the expertise of the appraisers.

Appraising and valuing a coin collection requires a strategic combination of methods that consider the unique attributes of each coin, market dynamics, and the broader numismatic landscape. While professional appraisals and grading services provide authoritative insights, collectors can complement these approaches with comparative analysis, online research, and networking within the numismatic community.

Chapter 5:

Curating and Preserving

As a devoted collector, the journey doesn't end with the acquisition of coins. Curating and preserving your numismatic treasures is a vital aspect of the hobby that ensures the longevity and integrity of your collection. In this chapter, we'll delve into the art of curating and preserving coins, exploring essential practices for coin storage and display, as well as detailing proper cleaning and preservation techniques.

Coin Storage and Display
Choosing the Right Storage Environment

The longevity of your coin collection hinges significantly on the environment in which it is stored. Creating an ideal storage environment involves considerations such as temperature, humidity, exposure to light, and protection against external elements.

1. **Temperature and Humidity Control**

Maintaining a stable temperature is crucial for preserving coins. Ideally, coins should be stored in an environment with a temperature between 60-70°F (15-21°C). Fluctuations in temperature can lead to the expansion and contraction of metal, potentially causing damage over time.

Similarly, controlling humidity is paramount. Aim for a humidity level between 50-55%. High humidity can promote corrosion, while low humidity may lead to the drying out of certain materials. Utilize dehumidifiers or humidifiers as needed to achieve optimal conditions.

2. **Protection Against Light**

Exposure to light, especially sunlight and ultraviolet (UV) light, can accelerate the aging process of coins. Direct sunlight can cause discoloration and fading, while UV light can be particularly damaging. Store your coins in dark, cool environments to shield them from light. If display is desired, consider utilizing UV-filtering glass or acrylic to minimize the impact of light exposure.

3. **Avoiding Pollutant**

Coins are susceptible to damage from airborne pollutants, which can lead to tarnishing and corrosion. Store your collection away from areas with high pollution levels or potential exposure to harmful gases. If displaying coins in an enclosed case, ensure proper ventilation to minimize the risk of pollutant accumulation.

Utilizing Proper Holders and Containers

The choice of holders and containers is instrumental in protecting your coins from physical contact, scratches, and environmental factors. Optimal storage solutions provide a secure and organized environment for your collection.

1. **Acid-Free Holders:** Select holders made from acid-free materials to prevent chemical reactions that can lead to degradation. Materials like Mylar or archival-quality paper are recommended for long-term storage. For individual coins, consider 2x2 holders made of safe materials.

2. **Coin Capsules:** Coin capsules, made from materials like acrylic, offer an additional layer of protection against physical contact and environmental elements. They come in various sizes to accommodate different coin denominations. Capsules also allow for easy inspection without the need to handle the coins directly.

3. **Albums and Holders:** For larger collections, albums with coin capsules or holders provide an organized and secure storage solution. Ensure that the albums are made from materials that do not contain PVC, as PVC can lead to chemical reactions causing damage to the coins.

4. **Desiccants for Humidity Control:** Place desiccants, such as silica gel packs, within your storage containers to control humidity. Desiccants help absorb excess moisture, creating a microenvironment that minimizes the risk of corrosion and mold growth. Regularly check and replace desiccants to ensure their effectiveness.

5. **Organizational Systems:** Implementing a systematic approach to organization is vital. Create an inventory that includes details such as coin type, mint year, and any special characteristics. This not only aids in keeping track of your collection but also assists in valuation and insurance purposes.

6. **Security Measures:** Consider security measures to protect your collection from theft or damage. Safes or safety deposit boxes offer secure storage options. Ensure that your insurance policy covers the full value of your collection and maintain a detailed inventory in case of unforeseen events.

7. **Regular Inspection:** Schedule regular inspections of your collection to identify any signs of deterioration or issues. Early detection allows for timely intervention, minimizing potential damage. During inspections, handle coins with clean hands or wear cotton gloves to prevent oil and dirt transfer.

Coin Display Strategies

While preservation is the primary focus of coin storage, displaying your collection can be a rewarding experience. Thoughtful display strategies not only showcase the beauty of your coins but also allow you to share your passion with others.

1. **Thematic Arrangement:** Consider arranging your coins thematically to create a visually engaging display. Group coins based on historical periods, geographic regions, or specific themes. This approach enhances the storytelling aspect of your collection, providing viewers with a cohesive narrative.

Example: French Louis d'Or If you have French Louis d'Or coins spanning different reigns, consider creating a display that showcases the evolution of these coins over time. Arrange them chronologically or based on the historical significance of each reign.

2. **Display Cases and Cabinets:** Enclosed display cases or cabinets provide protection against dust and environmental factors while allowing for easy viewing. Choose cases with UV-filtering glass or acrylic to minimize light exposure. Ensure that the interior is lined with materials that are safe for coins.

Example: German Mark German Marks, with their rich history, can be displayed in a dedicated case that protects them from physical contact and dust. Label each section of the case with information about the specific Mark, offering viewers insights into their significance.

3. **Floating Frames or Shadow Boxes:** Floating frames or shadow boxes create a unique and artistic display for coins. The transparent nature of these displays allows for a full view of the coins while adding a decorative element to your space.

4. **Rotating Displays:** For larger collections, rotating displays allow you to periodically showcase different sets of coins. This approach prevents overexposure to light and provides a refreshing viewing experience for both collectors and visitors.

Rotate your display based on themes or categories. For instance, dedicate a display period to coins featuring iconic figures, then switch to a theme centered around historical events. This dynamic approach keeps your collection visually stimulating.

5. **Interactive Displays:** Incorporate interactive elements into your display to engage viewers. Include informational cards or digital displays that provide details about each coin's history, design features, and cultural significance.

1. **Thermal Mounts and Frames:** Thermal mounts and frames protect coins from temperature and humidity fluctuations. These specialized mounts help create a stable microenvironment within the frame, reducing the risk of damage due to environmental factors.

Cleaning and Preservation Techniques

As a dedicated coin collector, the preservation of your numismatic treasures is paramount. While the act of cleaning coins is generally approached with caution, there are instances where gentle cleaning and proper preservation techniques can enhance the longevity and visual appeal of your collection.

Preservation is a delicate balance between maintaining a coin's historical authenticity and safeguarding it against the ravages of time. The following techniques are designed to help you navigate this balance and ensure the longevity of your numismatic treasures.

- **Understanding the Patina:** Patina, the thin layer that forms on the surface of coins over time, contributes to their character and is often desired by collectors. Before considering any cleaning, assess whether the coin's patina adds to its aesthetic appeal. Preserving the patina can maintain the coin's original appearance and historical value.
- **Conservation vs. Restoration:** Distinguishing between conservation and restoration is crucial. Conservation aims to stabilize and protect a coin without altering its original features, while restoration involves repairing or enhancing a coin's appearance. In numismatics, conservation is generally favored to preserve the coin's historical integrity.
- **Avoiding Over-Cleaning:** Over-cleaning can be detrimental to a coin's value and historical authenticity. The goal is to strike a balance between cleanliness and preservation. If a coin has attractive toning or patina, it's advisable to err on the side of caution and avoid aggressive cleaning methods that may remove these natural features.
- **Seeking Professional Advice:** For valuable or historically significant coins, seeking the expertise of a professional conservator is recommended. Conservators possess the knowledge and skills to assess the specific needs of a coin and implement appropriate preservation techniques without compromising its integrity.
- **Conservative Approach:** Adopt a conservative approach to preservation. It's often better to leave a coin in its natural state than risk damage through unnecessary cleaning. The numismatic community generally values coins that retain their original surfaces and features.

Cleaning Techniques

1. **Assessing the Need for Cleaning:** Before embarking on any cleaning process, carefully assess whether the coin requires cleaning. Dirt, grime, or contaminants on the surface may warrant cleaning, but if a coin is in good condition with no significant issues, consider leaving it untouched.

2. **Handling with Clean Hands or Gloves:** Always handle coins with clean hands to prevent the transfer of oils and dirt. Alternatively, wearing cotton gloves is advisable, especially when dealing with coins of higher value or rarity.

3. **Using Distilled Water:** Distilled water is a safe and gentle option for cleaning coins. Avoid tap water, as it may contain minerals that can leave deposits on the coin's surface. Place the coin in a small container, submerge it in distilled water, and let it soak briefly. Gently pat it dry with a soft cloth.

4. **Soft Brushes for Stubborn Dirt:** For coins with stubborn dirt or residue, soft-bristled brushes, such as camel hair brushes, can be employed. Lightly brush the surface to

dislodge dirt, taking care not to scratch the coin. Always brush in one direction to prevent potential abrasions.

5. **Avoiding Harsh Cleaning Agents:** Harsh chemicals and abrasive cleaning agents should be avoided at all costs. These substances can strip away the natural patina of a coin, diminishing its aesthetic appeal and historical character. Stick to mild, non-abrasive solutions if cleaning is necessary.

6. **Using Mild Soap Solutions:** In cases where dirt is adhered to the coin, a mild soap solution can be employed. Use a gentle dishwashing soap diluted in distilled water. Submerge the coin briefly and lightly scrub with a soft brush. Rinse thoroughly with distilled water and pat dry.

7. **Soft Erasers for Smudges:** Soft erasers, such as those made of gum or vinyl, can be used for smudges or light dirt. Gently rub the eraser on the affected area, avoiding excessive pressure. This method is effective for removing surface contaminants without compromising the coin's integrity.

8. **Conservator Assistance for Difficult Cases:** If a coin presents challenges that go beyond basic cleaning, seek the assistance of a professional conservator. Coins with intricate designs, delicate features, or those exhibiting signs of corrosion may require specialized expertise to ensure proper preservation.

9. **Preserving Original Surfaces:** The original surfaces of a coin are integral to its historical authenticity. Avoid interventions that compromise these surfaces, such as excessive cleaning or attempts to remove tarnish. Preserve the coin's original state to maintain its historical value.

Preservation Techniques

1. **Using Anti-Tarnish Strips:** Anti-tarnish strips, usually made of materials like activated charcoal, can be placed in storage containers to absorb pollutants and prevent tarnishing. These strips help maintain a controlled environment within the storage space.

2. **Applying Microcrystalline Wax:** Microcrystalline wax is a popular choice for coating coins to protect them from environmental elements. Apply a thin layer of wax using a soft brush or cloth, ensuring an even coverage. This method is effective for safeguarding coins from atmospheric pollutants.

3. **Interleaving with Archival Paper:** When storing coins in albums or holders, interleaving with archival-quality paper provides an additional layer of protection. Archival paper is acid-free and helps prevent contact between coins, reducing the risk of scratches.

4. **Humidity Control with Desiccants:** Desiccants, such as silica gel packs, play a dual role in preservation. Placing desiccants in storage containers helps control humidity, preventing conditions conducive to corrosion and mold growth. Regularly check and replace desiccants as needed.

5. **Avoiding PVC Holders:** Polyvinyl chloride (PVC) holders can lead to a chemical reaction known as "PVC damage," resulting in a greenish film on coins. Opt for holders made of PVC-free materials to prevent this type of damage. If PVC damage is suspected, consult a professional conservator.

6. **Consistent Storage Conditions:** Consistency in storage conditions is essential for preservation. Avoid exposing coins to extreme fluctuations in temperature and humidity. Regularly monitor the storage environment to ensure it aligns with optimal conditions.

7. **Avoiding Adhesive Materials:** When mounting or framing coins for display, avoid using adhesive materials that may leave residues or cause chemical reactions. Choose materials that are inert and won't negatively impact the coin's surface.

8. **Implementing Controlled Lighting:** If coins are displayed, control lighting conditions to prevent unnecessary stress on the artifacts. Use LED lighting with adjustable brightness to highlight details without emitting excessive heat. Ensure that coins are not exposed to direct sunlight.

Now, let's explore the preservation considerations for three culturally significant coins: the Russian Ruble, Chinese Cash Coin, and Japanese Yen.

1. **Russian Ruble**

The Russian Ruble, with its rich history dating back centuries, may exhibit various preservation challenges. Due to the diverse minting techniques and historical contexts of Russian coins, preservation efforts should prioritize stabilizing the current state while respecting the patina that contributes to their authenticity. The use of distilled water and soft brushes, if necessary, can be effective in addressing surface dirt without compromising the coin's integrity.

2. **Chinese Cash Coin**

Chinese Cash Coins, with their distinctive square holes and intricate designs, often have a unique patina that collectors value. Cleaning efforts should be approached cautiously, focusing on gentle methods to maintain the original surfaces. Soft brushes and distilled water can be used judiciously, with an emphasis on preserving the cultural and historical context embodied in each coin.

3. Japanese Yen

Japanese Yen coins, reflecting the artistry and symbolism of Japanese culture, require preservation techniques that honor their aesthetic appeal. Given the meticulous minting processes and symbolic elements, conserving the original surfaces and patina is crucial. Soft cloths and careful air-drying can be employed to maintain the integrity of these culturally significant coins.

Chapter 6:

Profiting from Coin Collecting

Entering the realm of coin collecting is not just a passion; for many, it's a strategic investment that can yield financial returns. In this comprehensive exploration, we'll delve into the strategies and nuances of profiting from coin collecting.

Buying and Selling Coins

The art of profiting from coin collecting involves a keen understanding of both the buying and selling processes. Whether you're acquiring coins for the love of the hobby or with an eye on potential future returns, strategic decisions at every stage can influence the profitability of your endeavors.

Buying Coins

1. **Research and Education**

The foundation of successful coin buying begins with thorough research and education. Familiarize yourself with the historical context, mintage figures, and notable variations of the coins you are interested in. Utilize reputable sources, numismatic literature, and online platforms to enhance your knowledge.

2. **Establishing Collecting Goals**

Clearly define your collecting goals before making any purchases. Are you collecting for historical significance, aesthetic appeal, or investment potential? Understanding your objectives guides your decision-making process and ensures that your acquisitions align with your overall vision for your collection.

3. **Identifying Reliable Sources**

Seek out reputable sources for purchasing coins. Established coin dealers, numismatic auctions, and well-regarded online platforms are avenues worth exploring. Establishing relationships with trustworthy dealers can provide access to a diverse range of coins and valuable insights into market trends.

4. Setting a Budget

Determine a budget for your coin acquisitions. Setting a realistic budget prevents impulsive purchases and aligns your collecting activities with your financial goals. Consider factors such as rarity, condition, and historical significance when establishing your budget for specific coins.

5. Grading and Authentication

Grading and authentication are critical aspects of buying coins, especially for collectors seeking quality and potential investment returns. Professional grading services assess the condition of coins, providing a standardized measure of quality. Authentication ensures the legitimacy of the coins, protecting buyers from potential forgeries.

6. Networking in the Numismatic Community

Engage with the numismatic community to expand your network and gain insights into potential buying opportunities. Numismatic forums, local clubs, and collector events offer platforms for connecting with fellow enthusiasts, sharing experiences, and discovering potential sources for acquiring coins.

7. Global Market Dynamics

Consider the global dynamics of the coin market, especially if you're interested in coins from different countries. Currency values, geopolitical factors, and economic conditions can influence the pricing and availability of coins. Stay informed about international trends to make informed decisions.

8. Coin Shows and Exhibitions

Attend coin shows and exhibitions to explore a wide array of coins, interact with dealers and collectors, and stay updated on market trends. These events provide opportunities for in-person assessments of coins and the chance to discover unique pieces that may not be readily available through other channels.

Selling Coins

1. Strategic Selling Goals

Similar to buying, selling coins benefits from well-defined goals. Determine whether you're selling to optimize returns, streamline your collection, or fund new acquisitions. Your selling strategy may vary based on these objectives.

2. Grading and Documentation

Presenting your coins in the best possible light requires attention to grading and documentation. If your coins are professionally graded, highlight these grades in your sales listings. Provide clear documentation, including provenance and any historical context that adds value to the coins.

3. Utilizing Online Platforms

Leverage online platforms for selling coins, offering a global reach to potential buyers. Auction websites, numismatic forums, and specialized online marketplaces provide convenient and accessible channels for selling coins. Include high-quality images and detailed descriptions to enhance your listings.

4. Establishing Fair Pricing

Determine fair and competitive prices for your coins. Research recent sales of similar coins to gauge market value. Consider factors such as rarity, condition, and historical significance when pricing your coins. Transparency in pricing builds trust with potential buyers.

5. Networking with Dealers

Build relationships with reputable dealers who may be interested in acquiring coins from your collection. Dealers often have insights into market demand and may provide fair offers for coins that align with their inventory needs.

6. Timing the Market

Be mindful of market cycles when selling coins. Strategic timing can impact the demand and pricing of certain coins. Consider the broader economic context and numismatic trends when deciding the optimal time to sell.

7. Auctions for Maximum Exposure

Participate in numismatic auctions for maximum exposure to potential buyers. Auctions attract a diverse audience, including serious collectors and investors. High-profile auctions can generate competitive bidding, potentially maximizing returns on your coin sales.

8. Diversifying Selling Channels

Diversify your selling channels to reach different segments of the market. While online platforms offer convenience, local coin shops, numismatic events, and auctions provide alternative avenues for selling coins. Tailor your approach based on the specific characteristics of your collection.

Illustrating the Global Landscape: Coins from Different Countries

1. **Indian Rupee**

The Indian Rupee, with its rich history and diverse coinage, presents unique opportunities for collectors and investors. The rupee has seen various designs and denominations over the years, reflecting India's cultural and historical evolution. Collectors interested in Indian coins may explore the vibrant numismatic market in India and international platforms that feature Indian currency.

2. **Mexican Peso**

Mexican Pesos, featuring iconic symbols such as the Aztec calendar and national heroes, hold significance in the numismatic world. The Mexican Mint produces a variety of denominations and designs, attracting collectors globally. Understanding the historical and cultural context of Mexican Pesos enhances the appeal for collectors seeking diverse and visually striking coins.

3. Australian Kangaroo Nugget

The Australian Kangaroo Nugget, also known as the Gold Nugget, is a distinctive coin produced by the Perth Mint. Featuring imagery related to Australia's iconic kangaroos and gold nuggets, this coin appeals to collectors fascinated by Australia's unique fauna and gold mining history. The international appeal of gold coins makes the Australian Kangaroo Nugget a sought-after addition to diverse collections.

4. Canadian Maple Leaf

The Canadian Maple Leaf, crafted by the Royal Canadian Mint, is renowned for its high purity and iconic maple leaf design. With variations in metal content, including gold, silver, platinum, and palladium, the Maple Leaf caters to a broad range of collectors and investors. The global recognition of the Maple Leaf contributes to its popularity on the international stage.

5. South African Krugerrand

The South African Krugerrand, introduced in 1967, holds historical significance as one of the first modern bullion coins. Named after Paul Kruger, a prominent figure in South African history, the Krugerrand is widely recognized and traded globally. Its association with gold makes it particularly appealing to those seeking precious metal investments.

Strategies for Maximizing Returns

Coin collecting, beyond being a passionate pursuit, often involves strategic considerations for maximizing returns. In this comprehensive exploration, we will delve into key strategies for maximizing returns in coin collecting, offering insights and actionable steps to enhance your numismatic success.

1. **Selectivity and Focus**

One of the foundational strategies for maximizing returns in coin collecting is selectivity. Instead of amassing a broad assortment of coins, focus on specific areas of interest or expertise. This targeted approach allows you to become an expert in certain types of coins, whether they are from a particular region, historical period, or feature specific design elements. Specialized knowledge enhances your ability to identify undervalued coins and make informed investment decisions.

Actionable Steps:

- Define your collecting niche based on personal interests or historical significance.
- Research and become well-versed in the specific attributes of coins within your chosen focus.
- Attend coin shows and engage with numismatic communities to stay updated on developments in your niche.

2. **Strategic Budgeting**

Establishing a well-defined budget is a crucial element of a successful coin collecting strategy. A budget not only prevents impulsive purchases but also ensures that your investments align with your financial goals. When allocating funds, consider factors such as rarity, historical significance, and market trends. A strategic budget allows you to diversify your collection while maintaining financial discipline.

Actionable Steps:

- Set a realistic and manageable budget for your coin collecting activities.
- Allocate funds based on your collecting objectives, giving priority to coins with potential for appreciation.
- Regularly review and adjust your budget in response to changes in financial circumstances or collecting goals.

3. Diversification

Diversifying your coin collection is a proven strategy for mitigating risks and maximizing returns. Instead of concentrating on a single type or era of coins, consider acquiring a diverse range that spans different regions, metals, and historical periods. Diversification safeguards your investment portfolio against the potential fluctuations in the value of specific coins.

Actionable Steps:

- Identify complementary categories within numismatics that align with your interests.
- Allocate a portion of your budget to coins with different denominations, metals, or cultural significance.
- Regularly assess your collection to ensure a balanced and diversified portfolio.

4. Grading and Authentication

Professional grading and authentication significantly enhance the marketability and value of coins. Third-party grading services provide standardized assessments of a coin's condition, adding transparency and credibility. Graded coins are often preferred by collectors and investors, and they tend to command higher prices in the market.

Actionable Steps:

- Send coins to reputable grading services to obtain professional assessments.
- Include information about the grade and authentication in your sales listings.
- Prioritize acquiring coins with recognized grades for your collection.

5. Market Timing

Timing is a crucial factor in the world of coin collecting. To maximize returns, be attentive to market cycles and trends. Consider making purchases during periods of lower demand when prices may be more favorable. Similarly, strategically time your sales to coincide with peaks in market demand for specific coins.

Actionable Steps:

- Stay informed about market trends through auction results, numismatic publications, and online forums.
- Monitor historical price movements and identify patterns that may influence your buying and selling decisions.
- Be flexible in your approach, adjusting your strategy based on the prevailing market conditions.

6. **Networking and Collaboration**

Building relationships within the numismatic community can open doors to valuable insights, opportunities, and collaborations. Engage with fellow collectors, dealers, and experts to share knowledge, exchange information, and potentially discover unique coins. Networking enhances your understanding of market dynamics and may lead to advantageous transactions.

Actionable Steps:

- Attend coin shows, conventions, and local numismatic events to connect with other enthusiasts.
- Join online forums and communities where collectors share experiences, tips, and market insights.
- Collaborate with dealers, collectors, and experts to enhance your numismatic network.

7. **Utilizing Online Platforms**

Embracing the digital landscape is essential for maximizing returns in the modern coin collecting market. Online platforms provide a global reach, connecting you with a diverse range of collectors and buyers. Utilize dedicated numismatic marketplaces, auction websites, and social media platforms to showcase your collection and facilitate transactions.

Actionable Steps:

- Create detailed and visually appealing listings for your coins on reputable online platforms.
- Engage with potential buyers through social media, forums, and online auctions.
- Leverage the convenience and accessibility of online platforms to broaden your reach.

8. Continuous Learning

Numismatics is a dynamic field with ongoing developments, discoveries, and market shifts. Commit to continuous learning by staying informed about industry trends, attending educational events, and engaging with experts. A proactive approach to learning positions you to make well-informed decisions that contribute to profit maximization.

Actionable Steps:

- Subscribe to numismatic publications and follow reputable websites for industry updates.
- Attend seminars, webinars, and workshops to deepen your knowledge.
- Actively engage in discussions with experts and fellow collectors to gain insights into emerging trends.

Maximizing returns in coin collecting involves a combination of passion, strategic thinking, and continuous learning. By adopting a selective focus, establishing a strategic budget, diversifying your collection, leveraging grading and authentication, timing your market activities, networking within the community, utilizing online platforms, and committing to continuous learning, you can craft a successful numismatic journey.

Chapter 7:

Rare Coins and Historical Significance

In the world of coin collecting, the pursuit of rare coins with unique historical significance elevates the hobby from a mere accumulation of currency to a captivating exploration of human history. Each rare coin becomes a tangible artifact, a portal to a specific moment in time, carrying the imprints of historical events, cultural shifts, and the stories of the people who once used and cherished them.

Coins with Unique Historical Context

Within this vast realm of numismatic exploration, certain coins stand out not only for their intrinsic beauty but also for the unique historical contexts they encapsulate. From the grandeur of Ancient Rome to the enigmatic allure of Ancient Egypt, the economic dynamism of Medieval Europe to the cultural richness of Ancient India and China, each coin tells a story that resonates across centuries.

1. **Ancient Roman Coin - Constantine the Great**

Among the most iconic figures in Roman history, Constantine the Great left an indelible mark, not only through his political and military achievements but also on the coinage of the Roman Empire. The Ancient Roman Coin featuring Constantine the Great serves as a numismatic tribute to the first Christian emperor. Minted during the 4th century AD, these coins often depict Constantine's portrait, showcasing the transition from paganism to Christianity in the Roman world. The issuance of coins with Christian symbols reflects the profound impact of Constantine's conversion and the pivotal role of Christianity in shaping the later Roman Empire.

2. Ancient Egyptian Ptolemaic Coin

The Ptolemaic Kingdom, a Hellenistic state that resulted from the victories of Alexander the Great, produced a distinctive series of coins that blended Greek and Egyptian elements. These Ancient Egyptian Ptolemaic Coins bear witness to the cultural fusion that characterized the Hellenistic period in Egypt. Featuring portraits of Ptolemaic rulers adorned with traditional Egyptian regalia, these coins reflect the delicate balance between Greek and Egyptian influences. The numismatic legacy of the Ptolemaic Kingdom serves as a testament to the cultural diversity and interplay that defined the ancient world.

3. Ancient Chinese Wu Zhu Coin

The Wu Zhu coin, an ancient Chinese currency used during various dynasties, holds a unique historical context within the rich tapestry of Chinese numismatics. With its square hole in the center and inscriptions that evolved over time, the Wu Zhu coin reflects the continuity and stability of Chinese monetary systems. From the Han Dynasty to the Tang Dynasty, these coins facilitated trade and economic transactions, providing a tangible connection to the enduring traditions of Chinese civilization. The evolution of inscriptions on Wu Zhu coins also serves as a linguistic and historical resource, tracing the shifts in political power and cultural influences.

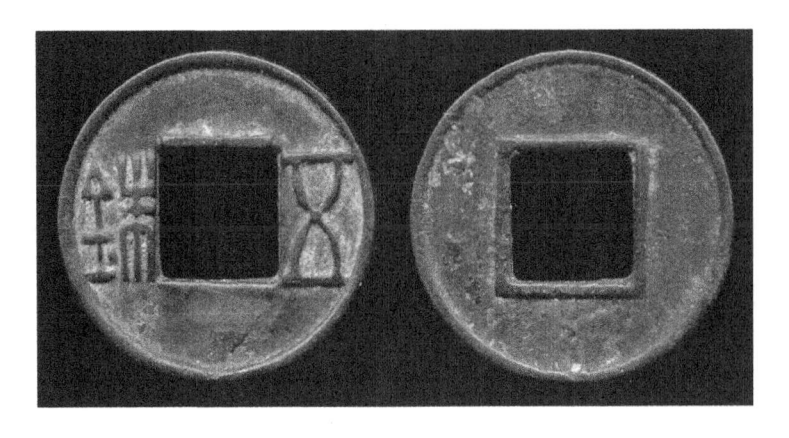

4. Ancient Indian Gupta Coin

The Gupta Empire, mostly mentioned to as the "Golden Age of India," produced coins that stand as exquisite examples of artistic and metallurgical excellence. The Ancient Indian Gupta Coins, featuring rulers like Chandragupta II, Kumaragupta, and Skandagupta, are characterized by intricate designs and sophisticated craftsmanship. These gold coins, known for their purity and aesthetic appeal, reflect the prosperity and cultural achievements of the Gupta period. The Gupta coinage provides insights into the economic vitality and artistic flourishing that marked this era in Indian history.

5. Ancient Byzantine Follis

The Byzantine Empire, with its capital in Constantinople, issued a distinctive coin known as the Follis. These Ancient Byzantine Follis coins, characterized by their large size and intricate designs, reflect the dynamic political and religious landscape of Byzantium. Featuring portraits of emperors and religious motifs, the Follis serves as a testament to the Byzantine Empire's endurance and adaptability. The inclusion of religious symbols on Byzantine coins, such as the Chi-Rho, underscores the close intertwining of religious and political authority in Byzantine society.

6. Medieval European Silver Penny

The medieval European Silver Penny, a widely circulated currency during the Middle Ages, played a crucial role in the economic life of medieval Europe. Minted by various European kingdoms and city-states, these coins bear the imprints of monarchs, heraldic symbols, and medieval iconography. The medieval Silver Penny reflects the decentralized nature of medieval Europe, where local authorities had the prerogative to issue their own coinage. Collecting these coins provides a glimpse into the diverse political and cultural landscapes of medieval Europe.

7. Medieval Islamic Dinar

The Islamic golden dinar, a currency that traces its origins to the early days of Islam, carries both historical and religious significance. The Medieval Islamic Dinar, characterized by its gold composition and calligraphic inscriptions, reflects the Islamic principles that shaped economic practices. The use of Arabic script on dinars often includes Quranic verses, emphasizing the integration of religious values into the economic sphere. Collectors of Medieval Islamic Dinars connect with a legacy of trade, scholarship, and cultural exchange that characterized the Islamic world during the medieval period.

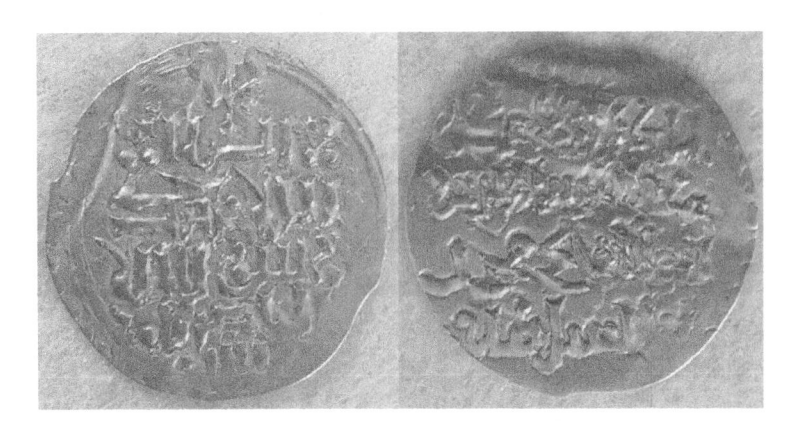

8. Spanish Colonial 8 Reales Cob

The Spanish Colonial 8 Reales Cob, often referred to as the "Piece of Eight," holds a noticeable place in the history of global trade and colonization. Minted in the Spanish colonies of the Americas, these silver coins became a widely accepted currency in international commerce. The Spanish Colonial 8 Reales Cob, with its irregular shape and distinctive markings, is a symbol of the economic interactions between the Old and New Worlds during the Age of Exploration. These coins, often associated with piracy and maritime adventures, carry the legacy of Spain's imperial ambitions and the complex history of the Americas.

9. Gold Rush Era U.S. Coin

The Gold Rush Era in the US, particularly during the mid-19th century, marked a transformative period in American history. Coins minted during this time, such as the Liberty Head designs, reflect the influx of gold from California and other gold-rich regions. The Gold Rush Era U.S. Coin captures the spirit of westward expansion, economic optimism, and the quest for wealth that defined this period. Collectors of these coins delve into the fascinating intersection of history, economics, and the pursuit of the American Dream.

10. Confederate States of America Coin

The coins issued by the Confederate States of America during the American Civil War carry a poignant historical context. Struck in limited quantities due to the economic challenges faced by the Confederate government, these coins are numismatic relics of a nation grappling with secession and conflict. The Confederate States of America Coin, whether the half dollar or cent, provides a tangible link to a tumultuous period in American history. Collectors of Confederate coins engage with the complexities and narratives of the Civil War, exploring the intersection of numismatics and historical memory.

Decoding the Cultural Significance

Numismatics goes beyond the realm of currency; it is a journey through time and culture, unlocking the stories embedded within metallic discs. Coins, as artifacts, are not merely tokens of trade; they are cultural touchstones that reflect the values, aspirations, and identities of the societies that produced them.

1. U.S. Trade Dollar

The U.S. Trade Dollar, minted from 1873 to 1885, holds a unique place in American numismatic history. Initially issued for trade with East Asia, particularly China, these silver dollars were intended to compete with the Mexican peso in the international market. The U.S. Trade Dollar reflects the economic ambitions of the US during the post-Civil War period and its desire to establish a presence in global trade. The coin's design features a depiction of Liberty with an Oriental-style headdress, symbolizing the intended destination of the coin. However, issues related to weight and fineness led to the Trade Dollar's eventual discontinuation. Collectors of U.S. Trade Dollars connect with a chapter in American history that underscores the intersection of commerce, diplomacy, and numismatics.

2. U.S. Standing Liberty Quarter

The U.S. Standing Liberty Quarter, minted from 1916 to 1930, represents a departure from traditional coin designs. Created by sculptor Hermon A. MacNeil, the coin features a dynamic portrayal of Liberty standing with one hand holding a shield and the other extending an olive branch. The design evokes a sense of resilience and readiness for defense, reflecting the US involvement in World War I during the coin's initial years of issuance. The U.S. Standing Liberty Quarter underwent modifications to address concerns about the visibility of Liberty's exposed breast, highlighting the sensitivity of cultural representations on coins. Collectors of this coin engage with the evolving artistic and cultural expressions of a nation in times of global conflict.

3. U.S. Barber Dime

The U.S. Barber Dime, named after its designer Charles E. Barber, was minted from 1892 to 1916. Featuring the profile of Liberty with a Phrygian cap, the coin is a reflection of the classical aesthetic prevalent during the late 19th and early 20th centuries. The U.S. Barber Dime captures the cultural ideals of the Gilded Age, with its emphasis on neoclassical motifs and artistic continuity. The coin's longevity and widespread circulation make it a numismatic window into the economic and cultural landscape of the turn of the century.

4. U.S. Mercury Dime

The U.S. Mercury Dime, minted from 1916 to 1945, stands as an iconic representation of American coinage. Despite its name, the coin's design features a depiction of Liberty wearing a winged cap, often mistaken for the Roman god Mercury. The U.S. Mercury Dime was minted during a period marked by both domestic and global challenges, including World War I and the Great Depression. The coin's imagery, evoking a sense of freedom and flight, resonates with the cultural sentiments of the early 20th century. Collectors of the Mercury Dime connect with a coin that encapsulates the spirit of an era characterized by resilience and innovation.

5. U.S. Washington Quarter

The U.S. Washington Quarter, first minted in 1932 to commemorate the bicentennial of George Washington's birth, holds a distinct place in American numismatics. Designed by sculptor John Flanagan, the coin features a profile of the nation's first president on the obverse and an eagle on the reverse. The U.S. Washington Quarter, with its enduring design, has undergone various modifications over the years, reflecting changes in minting technology and artistic interpretations. Collectors of the Washington Quarter witness the evolution of a coin that has become a symbol of national pride and historical commemoration.

6. U.S. Kennedy Bicentennial Half Dollar

The U.S. Kennedy Bicentennial Half Dollar, minted in 1976 to commemorate the bicentennial of the US, is a numismatic celebration of American history. Featuring a dual portrait of Presidents John F. Kennedy and Dwight D. Eisenhower on the obverse, and the Liberty Bell on the reverse, the coin marks a significant moment in the nation's journey. The U.S. Kennedy Bicentennial Half Dollar reflects the cultural and patriotic fervor surrounding the bicentennial celebrations, embodying a sense of unity and pride among Americans. Collectors of this coin engage with a tangible representation of the nation's commitment to its historical legacy.

7. U.S. Susan B. Anthony Dollar

The U.S. Susan B. Anthony Dollar, minted from 1979 to 1981 and again in 1999, is a coin with historical and cultural significance. Featuring a portrayal of women's suffrage advocate Susan B. Anthony, the coin was introduced to honor her contributions to the women's rights movement. The U.S. Susan B. Anthony Dollar, however, faced challenges in circulation due to its similarity in size and color to the U.S. quarter. Collectors of this coin engage with a numismatic representation of the ongoing struggle for gender equality and the recognition of pivotal figures in American history.

8. U.S. Sacagawea Dollar

The U.S. Sacagawea Dollar, first minted in 2000, pays homage to Sacagawea, the Shoshone guide and interpreter who accompanied the Lewis and Clark Expedition. Designed to celebrate Native American contributions to American history, the coin features a portrayal of Sacagawea with her infant son, Jean Baptiste. The U.S. Sacagawea Dollar, with its distinctive golden color, aims to honor the cultural diversity and historical narratives often overlooked in traditional coinage. Collectors of this coin participate in the ongoing dialogue about representation and inclusivity in numismatics.

9. Ancient Chinese Spade Money

Ancient Chinese Spade Money, dating back to the Zhou Dynasty (1046–256 BCE), holds a pivotal place in the history of Chinese currency. Shaped like agricultural spades or knives, these early forms of money were cast in bronze and served as a medium of exchange. The inscriptions on Ancient Chinese Spade Money often include details about the issuing authority or the purpose of the currency. Collectors of Spade Money engage with an ancient form of currency that reflects the agricultural and economic practices of early Chinese civilizations.

10. Ancient Greek Owl Tetradrachm

The Ancient Greek Owl Tetradrachm, minted in Athens during the 5th century BCE, is an iconic representation of ancient Greek coinage. Featuring the image of Athena's owl on the reverse and an image of the goddess Athena on the obverse, this coin symbolizes the cultural and artistic achievements of Athens during the classical period. The Ancient Greek Owl Tetradrachm, with its association with the goddess of wisdom, Athena, represents the intellectual and cultural vibrancy of ancient Greece. Collectors of this coin connect with a piece of numismatic history that transcends time, embodying the spirit of one of the world's greatest civilizations.

Decoding Cultural Significance: Strategies for Collectors

As collectors engage with coins carrying cultural significance, understanding the historical and cultural contexts becomes essential. Here are strategies for collectors to decode the cultural significance of coins:

- **Historical Research:** Conduct in-depth historical research to understand the circumstances, events, and cultural symbols associated with a particular coin. Historical context enhances the collector's appreciation for the narratives embedded within the coin's design and issuance.
- **Artistic Analysis:** Explore the artistic elements of a coin, including design motifs, symbols, and the work of the coin's designer. Artistic analysis provides insights into the cultural aesthetics and visual language of the time in which the coin was minted.
- **Sociopolitical Examination:** Consider the sociopolitical climate during the coin's issuance. Coins often reflect the political ideologies, power structures, and societal values prevalent at the time. Examining these aspects provides a nuanced understanding of the cultural significance of a coin.
- **Comparative Study:** Engage in comparative studies with other coins from the same era or region. Comparing coins allows collectors to identify common themes, variations, and shared cultural symbols that contribute to a broader understanding of numismatic contexts.
- **Collaborate with Experts:** Collaborate with numismatic experts, historians, and scholars who specialize in the cultural contexts of coins. Expert insights provide valuable perspectives and enhance the collector's ability to decode the nuanced cultural significance of specific coins.

Preserving Rare Coins

1. **Numismatic Conservation:** Engage in numismatic conservation practices to ensure the physical preservation of rare coins. Professional conservationists employ techniques to protect coins from environmental factors and potential deterioration. By prioritizing preservation, collectors contribute to safeguarding the tangible links to history.

2. **Historical Research:** Conduct in-depth historical research on each rare coin to uncover its specific historical context. Understanding the political, economic, and cultural circumstances surrounding the minting of a coin enhances its significance and adds layers of meaning to a collector's narrative.

3. **Cataloging and Documentation:** Implement thorough cataloging and documentation practices to create a detailed record of each rare coin in a collection. This includes information on minting dates, rulers, historical events, and any unique characteristics.

Comprehensive documentation ensures that the cultural and historical significance of each coin is preserved for future generations.

4. **Secure Storage:** Invest in secure storage solutions to protect rare coins from theft, environmental damage, and deterioration. Proper storage, including temperature and humidity control, helps maintain the integrity of coins over time. Safety deposit boxes, home safes, and specialized coin cabinets are popular options for collectors.

5. **Insurance Coverage:** Obtain insurance coverage for rare coin collections to provide financial protection in the event of theft, loss, or damage. Working with specialized insurers familiar with the nuances of numismatic collections ensures that collectors have adequate coverage for the unique value of their coins.

6. **Collaboration with Experts:** Collaborate with numismatic experts, historians, and curators to gain deeper insights into the historical and cultural contexts of rare coins. Expert opinions and appraisals contribute to a collector's understanding of the significance of their coins and help refine the narrative of a numismatic collection.

7. **Educational Initiatives:** Contribute to educational initiatives within the numismatic community and beyond. Sharing knowledge about rare coins and their historical contexts through exhibitions, lectures, and publications fosters a broader appreciation for the cultural significance of numismatic treasures.

Rare coins, with their unique historical contexts and cultural significance, are more than mere artifacts—they are storytellers, narrating the diverse and complex tales of human history. From the Ancient Roman Coin of Constantine the Great to the U.S. Sacagawea Dollar, each coin represents a chapter in the unfolding narrative of civilizations, trade, art, and societal evolution.

Chapter 8:

Conclusion and Next Steps

Reflecting on Your Coin Collecting Journey

As you stand at the intersection of history, art, and culture within the realm of coin collecting, it's time to pause and reflect on the captivating journey you've embarked upon. Numismatics is not just a hobby; it's a dynamic exploration of the past, a celebration of artistic expression, and a testament to the diversity of human civilizations. Your coin collecting journey has taken you through ancient empires, across centuries, and into the intricate narratives that lie within the small, metallic canvases you hold in your hands.

The Stories Encapsulated

Your coin collection is a testament to the stories encapsulated within each piece. Whether it's the Ancient Greek Silver Tetradrachm, the U.S. Kennedy Bicentennial Half Dollar, or the Ancient Chinese Spade Money, every coin speaks of a specific time, place, and cultural context. As a collector, you have become a steward of these stories, preserving the tangible links to our shared human history.

The Joy of Discovery

The joy of discovery is a perpetual source of satisfaction for coin collectors. Whether you find a rare piece at an antique shop, attend a coin show, or explore online markets, the thrill of stumbling upon a unique and valuable coin adds dynamism to your collecting journey. Keep the spirit of exploration alive, for each new coin holds the potential to unveil a fresh chapter in the vast narrative of numismatics.

Connecting with Community

Numismatics is more than an individual pursuit; it is a community-driven passion. The connections you forge with fellow collectors through numismatic forums, local clubs, and coin shows add a social dimension to your hobby. Sharing experiences, knowledge, and enthusiasm with like-minded individuals not only enhances your understanding of coins but also fosters a sense of camaraderie within the numismatic community.

The Evolution of Art

The artistic evolution of coins is a captivating aspect of your collection. From the simplicity of early mintings to the intricate designs of contemporary coins, you witness the visual language of different eras. Your collection becomes a condensed visual history, showcasing the prevailing styles, ideologies, and technological advancements that have shaped the world.

The Educational Journey

Coin collecting is an educational journey that goes beyond textbooks. The process of researching historical events, political climates, and symbolic meanings associated with each coin enhances your knowledge base. As you delve deeper into numismatics, you become not just a collector but a continual learner, uncovering the multifaceted layers of history and culture.

Continuing to Expand Your Collection

As one chapter of your coin collecting journey concludes, the allure of the next chapter beckons—a realm of unexplored possibilities, hidden gems, and undiscovered stories. Here are considerations and next steps to guide you as you continue to expand your collection:

Diversification of Themes and Eras

Consider diversifying your collection by exploring new themes, eras, or geographic regions. Delve into coins that represent uncharted territories within your numismatic interests. Whether it's ancient civilizations, medieval Europe, or modern commemorative coins, expanding your collection horizontally ensures a dynamic and comprehensive representation of numismatic history.

Specialized Knowledge Pursuit

Elevate your numismatic journey by deepening your knowledge in specific areas of interest. Specialized knowledge not only enhances your appreciation for the coins you collect but also positions you as an authority within the numismatic community. Whether it's delving into the intricacies of minting techniques, historical contexts, or the biographies of coin designers, specialized knowledge adds a layer of richness to your collecting experience.

Numismatic Literature Exploration

Immerse yourself in the vast world of numismatic literature. Books, journals, and online resources provide insights into the latest research, historical contexts, and market trends. Exploring numismatic literature enhances your understanding of the coins in your collection and guides you in making informed decisions as you continue to expand.

Engagement with Auctions and Shows

Participate in coin auctions and shows to uncover rare finds and connect with other collectors, dealers, and experts. These events offer opportunities to acquire unique coins, gain insights from experienced collectors, and stay informed about the evolving numismatic landscape. The thrill of auctions and the camaraderie of shows add a dynamic dimension to your collecting journey.

Collaboration and Mentorship

Consider collaborating with seasoned collectors or seeking mentorship within the numismatic community. Learning from experienced collectors can provide valuable insights, guidance, and access to resources. Mentorship fosters a sense of community and accelerates your growth as a collector.

Exploration of Emerging Trends

Stay attuned to emerging trends in numismatics, including new coin releases, innovative minting technologies, and evolving market preferences. Embracing contemporary developments ensures that your collection remains relevant and reflective of the ever-changing landscape of coin collecting.

Preservation and Documentation

Continue to prioritize the preservation and documentation of your collection. Adopt advanced preservation techniques, maintain accurate records, and consider leveraging digital platforms for cataloging and sharing your collection. Documentation ensures that the stories encapsulated within your coins are passed on to future generations.

Educational Initiatives

Share your passion and knowledge through educational initiatives. Whether it's organizing local exhibitions, contributing articles to numismatic publications, or conducting workshops, your expertise adds value to the numismatic community. Education becomes a reciprocal process, enhancing both your understanding and the collective knowledge within the community.

Adaptive Collecting Strategies

Remain adaptable in your collecting strategies. The numismatic landscape evolves, and being flexible allows you to navigate changes, seize opportunities, and refine your collection based on evolving interests and market dynamics. Adaptability ensures that your collection remains a reflection of your evolving passion for numismatics.

Legacy Planning

Consider legacy planning to ensure the continuity of your collection beyond your lifetime. Establish clear guidelines for the preservation, distribution, or donation of your collection. Collaborate with institutions, museums, or educational programs to secure the lasting legacy of your numismatic endeavors.

As you contemplate the next steps in your coin collecting journey, remember that each coin in your collection is a key that unlocks a unique story. The pursuit of these stories is not just a hobby; it is a lifelong adventure of discovery, learning, and connection. Numismatics, with its ability to transcend time and capture the essence of human history, offers a journey that is as boundless as your curiosity.

So, step forward with anticipation, curiosity, and the knowledge that your journey as a numismatist is a continuum—an ongoing exploration of the world encapsulated within metal, where every coin is a chapter waiting to be read, shared, and cherished. As you embark on the next chapter, may your collecting journey be adorned with new horizons, fascinating discoveries, and the enduring joy of numismatics.

Made in the USA
Las Vegas, NV
19 July 2024

92614357R00039